# D'Nealian®
## Home/School Activities:
### Manuscript Practice for Grades 1–3

# Donald N. Thurber

**Scott, Foresman and Company**
Glenview, Illinois    London

ANOTHER GOOD YEAR BOOK® WITH
D'NEALIAN® PRACTICE ACTIVITIES

## D'Nealian® Home/School Activities
### Cursive Practice for Grades 4–6
By Barbara Gregorich

Designed for teachers *and* parents, these reproducible,
ready-to-use activities supplement the popular *Scott,
Foresman D'Nealian® Handwriting Program*. You'll find a
variety of activities–125 in all–ranging from simple
cursive handwriting practice to challenging assignments
that develop thinking and writing skills. Each activity
includes clear, easy-to-follow directions, and each is flexible
enough to meet your students' varied needs and interests.
Special introductory material for parents and teachers
is included.

48 pages, paperback, ISBN 0-673-18176-6

For information about this or other Good Year Books®,
please contact your local school supply store or

> Good Year Books
> Scott, Foresman and Company
> 1900 East Lake Avenue
> Glenview, IL 60025

D'Nealian® Handwriting © 1981 Scott, Foresman and Company.
D'Nealian® is a registered trademark of Donald N. Thurber, licensed exclusively by
Scott, Foresman and Company, and is used here with permission. For a complete list of
D'Nealian® products, contact Scott, Foresman and Company, 1900 East Lake Avenue,
Glenview, IL 60025.

Copyright © 1986 Scott, Foresman and Company.
All Rights Reserved.
Printed in the United States of America.

ISBN 0-673-18535-4

16 17 18 19 - MAL - 99 98 97 96 95

No part of the book may be reproduced in any form or by any means, except those
portions intended for classroom use, without permission in writing from the publisher.

# Memo to Teachers and Parents

This book is intended for children at the lower primary level. It is assumed that they have had some writing experience. It is also assumed that they have some reading expertise, but you will undoubtedly have to help them read the instructions.

The purpose of this material is to enrich, maintain, or reinforce manuscript printing and provide a short lead-in to cursive writing.

Anyone who wants to work with children on handwriting must first understand a few points about how children learn and develop:

1 Children learn at different times, with different capacities, and in different ways. Don't expect child A to develop exactly as child B. Girls in the lower primary grades develop faster than boys, both physically and mentally. This is a normal pattern. Expect to see girls as a group outperform boys as a group at the beginning level.

2 Be patient with slower learners. Give them more time, expect less finished work, and don't pressure. This is a diffi-cult point to follow but is essential for their development.

3 *Success produces more success while failure begets failure.* The twenty-six lower-case and twenty-six uppercase letters give the child plenty of chances to succeed at handwriting and give you plenty of chances to praise work well done.

4 Print manuscript is more legible and easier to write than cursive, and it can be done just as fast. There is thus no real need to rush the child into connected writing. A child who has mastered the printing script, using correct size, spacing, and slant, can easily change to cursive writing.

5 Many of the exercises are related to reading and language arts. This helps the child learn more than penmanship from the lessons. Because the material spans the mid-first-grade to third-grade reading levels, however, do not expect every child to complete everything without help.

# How to Teach the Letters

The letters *a*, *c*, *d*, *e*, *g*, *o*, and *s* should be taught as a group. They all begin about the same and are made with nearly the same rhythm. The letter *e* starts differently, but, after making the upstroke, the child completes the letter by just wrapping a *c* around the upstroke.

D'Nealian™ Handwriting uses audio instructions to help the child remember stroke direction. Air-writing (be very careful to synchronize finger movements with audio directions), sandbox writing, making letters with clay, and tracing on dusty or chalky surfaces are good techniques to help reinforce directionality.

Draw a large *a* on the chalkboard, on cardboard, or on paper. Point out where you begin (about the two o'clock position), and describe how you are forming the letter in a rhythmic manner. Do this by raising or lowering the pitch of your voice or stretching out a word sound to coincide with your hand movement: "Letter *a*—around, down [lower your tone of voice], close up [raise your tone of voice], down [lower], and a monkey tail [stretch out the last word]."

Trace over the letter *a* several times, each time describing what you are doing *as you do it*. Then have the child start at the correct position and trace over the letter while you describe the child's movement as he or she shapes the letter.

The audio directions for each letter are marked by stars on the practice pages. Go over these audio directions, helping the child to read them. When the child can say them without your help, he or she should then, with a pencil, trace over the model letters, simultaneously saying the stroke directions aloud.

Most children who have handwriting problems have them because they use improper starting points and stroke directions. It is essential that the child be made aware of the correct starting point and the proper direction for making each letter.

Children should be able to form in a row three letters of comparable size, slant, and shape. Each child must reach this goal to master the printing of each different letter. Practicing one letter in a few groups of three usually leads to good letter formation. Writing a whole page of letters, as a method of improvement, is boring, produces fatigue, and often evokes a distaste for the learning task.

There is another form of reinforcement that helps some children learn to write. It involves a combination of audio directions and touch. You simply use your finger to trace the letter on the child's hand, arm, or back, and you say the audio directions in exact synchronization with the movements that form the letter. The child can thus connect what he or she hears with the physical feel of how the letter is formed. The learner then traces on your hand, saying the directions while forming the letter. If the child forms the letter properly, you then test the permanence of the reinforcement: you say the audio directions but trace an inappropriate design or letter on the child's hand. If the learner responds that the oral directions don't match the feel of the letter, you can be sure that he or she has the formation of the letter fixed in memory.

Letters are introduced with a right-hand slant because this is the most common natural slant. However, no two people write exactly alike; some writers naturally write straight up and down while others may backslant. Any slant is acceptable—right-hand, left-hand, or vertical—but whichever slant the child develops, the child must use it consistently. Writing with inconsistently slanted letters is not acceptably legible.

*a d*

Write a group of three **a**'s in each box. Start at the dot, and follow the arrow. Say the directions out loud as you write the letters.

☆ **Around, down, up, down, and a monkey tail.** ☆

Write groups of **a**'s. Remember which way the arrow points. Remember to start at the dot.

Write a group of three **d**'s in each box. The **d** starts just like letter **a**. Letter **d** is a tall or sky letter. It takes two spaces. Start at the dot, and follow the arrow.

☆ **Around, down, up high, down, and a monkey tail.** ☆

Write three more groups of letter **d**'s. Remember which way the arrow points.

Write the words **dad** and **add**.

*dad*          *dad*
*add*          *add*

From D'Nealian™ Home/School Activities: Manuscript Practice for Grades 1–3, Copyright © 1986 Scott, Foresman and Company.

NAME

*o g*

Write a group of three **o**'s in each box. Start at the dot, and follow the arrow.

☆ **Around, down, up, and close.** ☆

Write three more groups of letter **o**'s. Start at the dot, and remember the arrow.

Write groups of three **g**'s. Start at the dot, and follow the arrow. The **g** begins like letters **a**, **d**, and **o**, but it goes under water.

☆ **Around, down, up, down, and a fishhook under water.** ☆

Write more groups of letter **g**'s. Keep the back straight when going under water.

Write the words below. Watch your slant.

*dog*
*odd*

*good*
*do*

 From D'Nealian™ Home/School Activities: Manuscript Practice for Grades 1–3, Copyright © 1986 Scott, Foresman and Company.

c e

Write a group of three **c**'s in each box. Start at the dot, and follow the arrow.

⭐ **Curved start, around, down, up, and stop.** ⭐

Write groups of three **e**'s. Start with a curved line up, and wrap a **c** around it.

⭐ **Curved line up, around, down, up, and stop.** ⭐

Write the words below. Watch your slant.

cage        dodge
edge        egg
deed        doe
good        age
dad         add
do          dead

**s i**

Write groups of three **s**'s. Start at the dot, and follow the arrow.

⭐ **Curved start, around left, and a snake tail.** ⭐

Write more groups of **s**'s. Remember the arrow. Start at the dot.

Write the words.

*seed*    *eggs*

*gas*    *geese*

*case*    *soda*

Write groups of three **i**'s. Start at dot 1. Dot 2 is a dot you must add.

⭐ **Down and a monkey tail. Add a dot.** ⭐

Write the words.

*ice*    *dad*

*side*    *dogs*

*did*    *sea*

*is*    *die*

*b k*

When you write the tall letters **b**, **d**, **f**, **h**, **k**, **l**, and **t**, make them twice the size of most other letters. This means taller, not wider. Write groups of letter **b**'s. Start at the dot, and follow the arrow.

⭐ **High start, down, around, up into a tummy.** ⭐

*b b b     b b b*

Remember the arrow. Start at the dot.

Write the words.

*bag          good*
*beg          big*
*bead         bed*

Write groups of letter **k**'s. Start at the dot, follow the arrow, and make **k** two spaces tall.

⭐ **High start, down, up, small tummy, and a monkey tail.** ⭐

*k k k     k k k*

Write the words below. Watch your slant and letter spacing.

*kick         bake*
*bike         cake*

From D'Nealian™ Home/School Activities: Manuscript Practice for Grades 1-3, Copyright © 1986 Scott, Foresman and Company.

**5**

*l h*

Write groups of letter **l**'s. Do a good job because you will use **l** to make a **t**. Start at the dot.

⭐ **High start, down, and a monkey tail.** ⭐

Write the words below. Be certain to make the back of letter **l** straight.

*lake*
*like*

*glass*
*close*

Write groups of letter **h**'s. Keep the down line straight, not like these: *h  h* . Remember to start at the dot. Follow the arrow.

⭐ **High start, down, up, and a hump with a monkey tail.** ⭐

Write the words below.

*hook*
*look*

*hide*
*head*

 From D'Nealian™ Home/School Activities: Manuscript Practice for Grades 1–3, Copyright © 1986 Scott, Foresman and Company.

$f\ t$

Write groups of letter **f**'s. Begin with a small line curving up, and then go straight down. It looks like a candy cane so far. Then make a line across. Start at the dot, and follow the arrow.

☆ **Curved high start, around, and down. Cross.** ☆

Do a few more. Keep the back of **f** straight.

Write the words below.

*food*          *feel*

*face*          *fill*

Write groups of letter **t**'s. The **t** is made like letter **l** at the start, but it has a line across in the middle.

☆ **High start, down, and a monkey tail. Cross.** ☆

Like **b**, **d**, **f**, **h**, and **l**, the **t** has a straight back. Cross it in the middle, not like these: *t t* . Write the words below.

*tickle*          *take*

*little*          *feet*

*kite*          *tall*

$m$ $n$

Write groups of letter **m**'s. Start at the dot, and follow the arrow.

⭐ **Down, up, hump, hump, and a monkey tail.** ⭐

Remember the arrow, and start at the dot. Do not make your **m** too wide or too thin like these: $m$ $m$

Write the words below.

*made*      *mile*

*mom*      *magic*

*mind*      *moose*

Write groups of letter **n**'s. Letter **n** has only one hump.

⭐ **Down, up, hump, and a monkey tail.** ⭐

Write the words below.

*note*      *nine*

*nose*      *need*

*nice*      *nest*

  From D'Nealian™ Home/School Activities: Manuscript Practice for Grades 1–3, Copyright © 1986 Scott, Foresman and Company.

r v

Write three groups of letter **r**'s. Start at the dot, and follow the arrow.

⭐ **Down, up, and a roof.** ⭐

Write groups of **r**'s. Letter **r** is made almost like letter **n**, but it does not end with a tail.

Write the words below.

red          recess
roam         rain

Write groups of letter **v**'s. Start at the dot, and follow the arrow.

⭐ **Slant right down, slant right up.** ⭐

When writing letter **v**, do not make it too wide or too thin like these: ⌣ v . Write more **v**'s.

Write the words below. Watch the size, slant, and spacing of your letters.

vacation
village
valentine

*q u*

Write groups of letter **q**'s. Make **q** like letter **g** but with a backward fishhook. The fishhook touches the line below the water. Start at the dot, and follow the arrow.

⭐ **Around, down, up, down, and a backward fishhook under water.** ⭐

Write groups of letter **u**'s. Follow the arrow. Whenever you spell an English word beginning with **q**, you must always use a **u** after the **q**.

⭐ **Down, over, up, down, and a monkey tail.** ⭐

Write the words below. Don't forget to always use **u** after **q**. Did you notice **q** starts like letters **a**, **c**, **d**, **g**, and **o**?

| quick | quilt |
| quiet | queen |
| use | quit |
| until | uncle |

Write letters **g**, **q**, **a**, **c**, **d**, and **o** three times each.

| g | q | a |
| c | d | o |

*j p*

Write a group of letter **j**'s in each box. Like letter **i**, the **j** has a starting dot and a dot you must add.

⭐ **Down, and a fishhook under water. Add a dot.** ⭐

Write groups of **j**'s. Keep the line straight as you slant down under water. Letter **j** does not look like these: *j ɔ ʝ*

Write the words. Watch your spacing and slant.

*joke*
*jam*

*jail*
*join*

Write groups of letter **p**'s.

⭐ **Down under water, up, around, and a tummy.** ⭐

Practice writing the words below.

*page*
*papa*

*people*
*pad*

_w x_

Write three groups of letter **w**'s. Start at the dot, and follow the arrow.

☆ **Down, over, up, down, over, up.** ☆

Letter **w** is made like two **u**'s together. Be careful not to make it too wide or too thin: _w w_

These are hard words to always get right, so write them right now.

_what_      _which_

_where_      _while_

Write three groups of letter **x**'s. Make a line with a monkey tail first: _ı_. Then finish with a slanted straight line: _／_ There are two parts to letter **x**.

☆ **Slant down, and a monkey tail. Cross with a slant.** ☆

Small letter **x** and capital letter **X** are made the same way except that one is larger. Make groups of small **x**'s. Remember the arrow. Start at the dot.

Write these words for practice.

_wax_      _ax_      _exit_

 From D'Nealian™ Home/School Activities: Manuscript Practice for Grades 1–3, Copyright © 1986 Scott, Foresman and Company.

**NAME**

y z

Write groups of letter **y**'s. Start at the dot, and follow the arrow. Use two full spaces as you do when making **g, j, p,** and **q**.

⭐ **Down, over, up, down under water, and a fishhook.** ⭐

Write groups of **y**'s. Be certain to keep the back of the **y** straight. Do not make it like these: y y y

Write the words below.

young          yell
yard           yarn

Write groups of letter **z**'s. Letter **s** starts to the left, but **z** starts to the right. Start at the dot, and follow the arrow.

⭐ **Over, slant down, over.** ⭐

Write the words below.

zoo            zip
zero           zoom

# Reverse Words

Each word below can be written backward to make a new word. The first one has been done for you. Remember, sky letters take two spaces. Be careful of your slant and spacing.

| | |
|---|---|
| *was saw* | *stop* |
| *pit* | *buh* |
| *not* | *tap* |
| *nap* | *pool* |
| *on* | *pins* |
| *but* | *star* |
| *rat* | *bag* |
| *pot* | *dam* |
| *pal* | *dab* |
| *pin* | *ten* |
| *won* | *bat* |

Use this space to practice words you're not pleased with.

| | | | |
|---|---|---|---|
| | | | |
| | | | |
| | | | |
| | | | |

 From D'Nealian™ Home/School Activities: Manuscript Practice for Grades 1–3, Copyright © 1986 Scott, Foresman and Company.

# Numbers 0–20

Look at the number names below.

| | | |
|---|---|---|
| zero | seven | fourteen |
| one | eight | fifteen |
| two | nine | sixteen |
| three | ten | seventeen |
| four | eleven | eighteen |
| five | twelve | nineteen |
| six | thirteen | twenty |

Write the number name by each number. Watch your slant, size, and spacing.

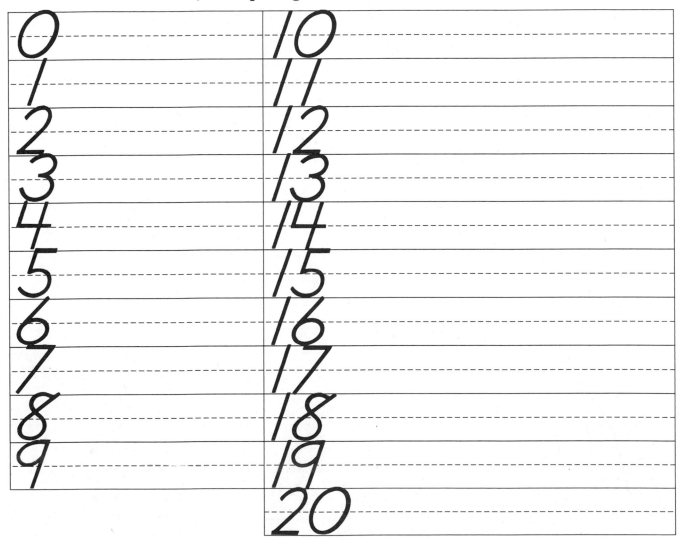

# Compound Words

Put the words together to make new words. The first one has been done for you.

| | | |
|---|---|---|
| high | highchair | corn |
| pop | | body |
| every | | selves |
| them | | chair |

| | | |
|---|---|---|
| grand | | house |
| green | | milk |
| up | | stairs |
| butter | | son |

| | | |
|---|---|---|
| base | | plane |
| air | | one |
| some | | ball |

| | | |
|---|---|---|
| my | | bird |
| foot | | self |
| after | | noon |
| blue | | ball |

 From D'Nealian™ Home/School Activities: Manuscript Practice for Grades 1–3, Copyright © 1986 Scott, Foresman and Company.

# Blends

Using the blend at the top of the box, write the words. Watch your spacing and slant.

## ch

air
ild
ain

## st

reet
ring
ar

## bl

ue
ock
ack

## th

ree
ing
in

## cl

ock
ean
ear

## sh

ut
eep
ine

## ch

urch
ild
eese

## dr

aw
ive
ink

From D'Nealian™ Home/School Activities: Manuscript Practice for Grades 1–3, Copyright © 1986 Scott, Foresman and Company.

# Antonyms

Antonyms are words that mean the opposite of each other. Some are **day** and **night**, **happy** and **sad**, and **up** and **down**. Match the opposites. The first one has been done. Watch your spacing, slant, and letter size.

| | | | |
|---|---|---|---|
| sharp | sharp | dull | right |
| in | | | out |
| left | | | light |
| dark | | | dull |
| soft | | | yes |
| day | | | night |
| no | | | hard |
| push | | | light |
| wet | | | pull |
| heavy | | | dry |
| lost | | | found |
| flat | | | short |
| tall | | | round |
| mom | | | frown |
| smile | | | dad |

 From D'Nealian™ Home/School Activities: Manuscript Practice for Grades 1–3, Copyright © 1986 Scott, Foresman and Company.

# Silent e Endings

Write each word, but leave off the silent ending **e**. Find the new words.

| | |
|---|---|
| tube | paste |
| pine | rate |
| use | shine |
| fate | huge |
| cape | hope |
| mane | theme |
| bite | quite |
| cube | globe |
| kite | note |
| plane | mate |
| robe | tote |

Practice words to improve on.

## C S

Write groups of capital C's. Make three in each box. Start at the dot, and follow the arrow. Be sure to use two full spaces for all your capital letters.

☆ **Curved high start, around, down, up, and stop.** ☆

Write the words below.

| Come | Cry | Cats |
|------|-----|------|
| Cart | Cabin | Cash |

Write three groups of capital S's. Use two full spaces. Start at the dot, and follow the arrow.

☆ **Curved high start, around left, and a snake tail.** ☆

Write the words below.

| Sister | Sugar | Smog |
|--------|-------|------|
| Slow | Street | Some |

 From D'Neallan™ Home/School Activities: Manuscript Practice for Grades 1–3, Copyright © 1986 Scott, Foresman and Company.

O O Q

Write groups of capital **O**'s. Capital **O** is made just like small **o**. Follow the arrow. Use two spaces for all capital letters.

⭐ Curved high start, around, down, up, and close. ⭐

Write the words.

| Over | Only | Once |
|------|------|------|
| Order | Often | Ouch |

Write three groups of capital **Q**'s. Make **Q** like letter **O**, only add a monkey tail.

⭐ Curved high start, around, down, up, and close. Add a monkey tail. ⭐

Write the **Q** words. Always use letter **u** after **Q** when spelling English words.

| Quick | Quit | Quart |
|-------|------|-------|
| Queen | Quiet | Quiz |

V U

Write groups of capital letter **V**'s. Capital **V** is just like small **v** except that it takes two spaces.

⭐ **Slant right down, slant right up.** ⭐

Write these words, beginning each with a capital **V**.

Valley | Very | Violet

View | Van | Vanilla

Write groups of capital **U**'s. Start at the dot, and follow the arrow. Do not make **U** too wide or too thin: U u

⭐ **High start, down, over, up high, down, and a monkey tail.** ⭐

Write the words below.

Umbrella
Upstairs
Uniform

Write the sentence.

Umpires use umbrellas.

 From D'Nealian™ Home/School Activities: Manuscript Practice for Grades 1–3, Copyright © 1986 Scott, Foresman and Company.

*X Z*

Capital **X** is made just like small **x**. Be careful not to make it too wide. Follow the first arrow, and then add the cross line.

☆ **High start, slant right down, and a monkey tail. Cross with a slant.** ☆

Write these words.

*Xmas* | *X-ray*

Letter **Z** goes to the right with the first line, in this direction: ⟶. Make groups of letter **Z**'s. Start at the dot, and follow the arrow.

☆ **Over right, slant left down, over right.** ☆

Write the words.

*Zebra* | *Zoo* | *Zero*

Write each letter three times.

*C* | *O*
*Q* | *S*
*V* | *U*
*X* | *Z*

*P J*

Write groups of capital letter **P**'s. Capital **P** is made just like small **p**. Keep its back straight, not like these: *P P*

☆ **High start, down, up, and a tummy.** ☆

*P P P    P P P*

Write the words and sentence.

*Pop          Pet          Puppy*

*Pam likes Popsicles.*

Capital letter **J** is made like small **j** except that it has no dot at the top.

☆ **High start, down, and a fishhook.** ☆

*J J J    J J J*

Write the words and sentence.

*Joke        Jelly        Juice*

*Jack broke the jar.*

 From D'Neallan™ Home/School Activities: Manuscript Practice for Grades 1–3, Copyright © 1986 Scott, Foresman and Company.

## HI

Capital letter **H** takes three strokes to make. First slant down / , then make another slant line / , and then cross in the middle − . Don't make **H** too wide.

☆ **High start, down. High start, down. Middle bar across.** ☆

Write the words.

| High | Held | Help |
|------|------|------|
| Hill | Home | Hold |

Letter **I** also uses three strokes. First slant down, then add a top crossbar, and then add a bottom crossbar.

☆ **High slant down. Cross top. Cross bottom.** ☆

Write these practice words.

| Inches | Inside | Itch |
|--------|--------|------|
| Island | Invite | Into |

From D'Nealian™ Home/School Activities: Manuscript Practice for Grades 1–3, Copyright © 1986 Scott, Foresman and Company.

*A B*

Write groups of capital **A**'s. It takes three strokes to make **A**. Start at the dot, and follow the numbers and arrows.

⭐ **High start, slant left down. Same high start, slant right down. Cross.** ⭐

Write the sentences.

*Amy lives in Ann Arbor.*

*U.S.A. means America.*

Write groups of capital **B**'s. Be certain to make the **B** have two tummies the same size, not like these: *B B*

⭐ **Slant down, up on same line, around halfway, around again.** ⭐

Write the sentences.

*Ben bumped Bill's bike.*

*Bob hugged Aunt Betty.*

 From D'Nealian™ Home/School Activities: Manuscript Practice for Grades 1-3, Copyright © 1986 Scott, Foresman and Company.

D E

Write groups of capital **D**'s. Start at the dot, and follow the arrow.

⭐ **Slant down, up on same line, tumble over.** ⭐

Write the sentences below. Watch your word and letter spacing. Capital and tall letters take two spaces.

*Donald Duck is funny.*

*Dr. Doolittle likes dogs.*

Write groups of capital **E**'s. Start at the dot, and follow the two arrows.

⭐ **High start, over left, down, over right. Middle bar across.** ⭐

Each word is a person's name. Write the words.

| *Earl* | *Ellen* | *Effie* |
|--------|---------|---------|
| *Edie* | *Eric* | *Elmo* |

W Y

Write groups of capital **W**'s. Use two spaces, and watch your slant.

☆ **High start, slant right down, slant right up, slant right down, slant right up.** ☆

Write the sentence below.

*We went to Windsor.*

Write groups of capital **Y**'s. Take special care not to make the top part too wide.

☆ **High start, slant right halfway. High start, slant left down.** ☆

Write the words below.

*You*     *Your*     *Yes*

If your **W** and **Y** are too wide, practice them again.

**M R**

Write groups of letter **M**'s. Do not make **M** too wide. The middle of **M** touches the center line. Space carefully.

⭐ **High start, down. Same high start, slant down halfway, slant up, down.** ⭐

M M M M    M M M

Write the state name words below.

Maine
Maryland
Missouri
Michigan
Montana

Write groups of letter **R**'s. Start at the dot, and follow the arrow. Watch your slant, size, and spacing.

⭐ **High start, down, up, around halfway, slant down, and a monkey tail.** ⭐

R R R    P P P

Write the sentences below.

Mister Rogers is nice.

Rick likes to race.

N T

Write groups of capital **N**'s. Watch your slant. You must lift your pencil to make **N**.

⭐ **High start, down. Same high start, slant down, then up.** ⭐

Write the poem called "November" below.

No shade, no shine,

No butterflies, no bees,

No fruits, no flowers,

No leaves, no birds,

November!

Write groups of capital **T**'s. This letter is easy.

⭐ **High start, down. Cross.** ⭐

Write the words below.

There          Thin

From D'Nealian™ Home/School Activities: Manuscript Practice for Grades 1–3, Copyright © 1986 Scott, Foresman and Company.

F G

Write groups of capital **F**'s. Don't make **F** too far out like this: F . Start at the dot, and follow the arrow.

⭐ **High start, over left, down. Middle bar across.** ⭐

F F F

Many place names start with the word **Fort**. State and city names always begin with a capital letter. Write the city names. Begin each word with a capital letter.

fort dodge
fort meyers
fort worth

Write groups of capital **G**'s. Make **G** like capital **C**, only put a bar on the end.

⭐ **Curved high start, around, down, up, and over left.** ⭐

G G G

Write the city names below.

Glen        Garner        Goshen

Write the sentence below.

Go to Grove City.

K L

Write groups of letter **K**'s. You have to lift your pencil to make a **K**.

☆ **High start, down. High start, slant halfway, slant down, and a monkey tail.** ☆

K  K  K  |  |  |  |  |  |

Write the words below. All are bird names.

Kiwi

Kingfisher

Kea

Kittiwake

Kestrel

Kite

Write groups of letter **L**'s. Keep the bottom of **L** straight.

☆ **High start, down, and over right.** ☆

L  L  L  |  |  |  |  |  |

Write the animal words.

| Lion | Leopard | Lynx |
| --- | --- | --- |
| Lobster | Lizard | Lamb |

 From D'Neallan™ Home/School Activities: Manuscript Practice for Grades 1–3, Copyright © 1986 Scott, Foresman and Company.

# Oceans, Lakes, and Rivers

Write the names of the oceans, lakes, and rivers in the right boxes. Use a capital letter to begin each name. Watch your slant, size, and spacing.

## Oceans

Atlantic Ocean

Lake Superior

Mississippi

Pacific Ocean

Lake Huron

## Lakes

Colorado

Missouri

Great Salt Lake

Indian Ocean

Lake Erie

Platte

Lake Michigan

Lake Ontario

## Rivers

# Synonyms

Synonyms are different words that mean the same thing.
Match synonyms, and write both words. Be careful of word and
letter spacing.

| | | |
|---|---|---|
| tame | | quick |
| dish | | gentle |
| fast | | plate |
| push | | street |
| road | | shove |

| | | |
|---|---|---|
| talk | | leap |
| jump | | papa |
| dad | | speak |
| tot | | grin |
| smile | | child |

| | | |
|---|---|---|
| jolly | | mug |
| zero | | happy |
| cup | | none |
| say | | twist |
| bend | | tell |

  From D'Nealian™ Home/School Activities: Manuscript Practice for Grades 1–3, Copyright © 1986 Scott, Foresman and Company.

# Number Names

Look at the number names below.

| | | | | | |
|---|---|---|---|---|---|
| 1 | one | 7 | seven | 40 | forty |
| 2 | two | 8 | eight | 50 | fifty |
| 3 | three | 9 | nine | 60 | sixty |
| 4 | four | 10 | ten | 70 | seventy |
| 5 | five | 20 | twenty | 80 | eighty |
| 6 | six | 30 | thirty | 90 | ninety |

Write the number names by the numbers. Use a hyphen between two number names to make up a new number name. The first one has been done for you.

40 forty  +  2 two  =  42          *forty-two*

60 sixty  +  1 one  =  61

50 fifty  +  5 five  =  55

90 ninety  +  3 three  =  93

30 thirty  +  9 nine  =  39

40 forty  +  8 eight  =  48

70 seventy  +  2 two  =  72

90 ninety  +  6 six  =  96

80 eighty  +  4 four  =  84

20 twenty  +  7 seven  =  27

60 sixty  +  6 six  =  66

# Contractions

A contraction is a short way to write two words. Write the words that match each contraction. Keep the same slant, size, and spacing as you write them.

| | | |
|---|---|---|
| *it's* | | I am |
| *isn't* | | we have |
| *you're* | | he is |
| *we're* | | they have |
| *I'm* | | you will |
| *he's* | | it is |
| *didn't* | | was not |
| *you'll* | | you are |
| *she'll* | | is not |
| *that's* | | did not |
| *I've* | | that is |
| *don't* | | we are |
| *they've* | | I have |
| *wasn't* | | let us |
| *let's* | | she will |
| *we've* | | do not |

 From D'Nealian™ Home/School Activities: Manuscript Practice for Grades 1–3, Copyright © 1986 Scott, Foresman and Company.

# Word Families

Once you learn a word, often you can use it as part of another word. The word **out** can be used in many ways. Write the **out** family words. Then do **ump** words.

| | | |
|---|---|---|
| out | scout | outfit |
| spout | about | stout |
| outlaw | sprout | outlet |
| snout | outdoor | shout |

| | | |
|---|---|---|
| ump | jump | bump |
| pump | lump | thump |
| dump | umpire | plump |
| clump | stump | grump |

# Months of the Year

Write the months of the year, in order. Use a capital letter to begin each month's name.

| | |
|---|---|
| *January* | |
| *February* | |
| *March* | |
| *April* | |
| *May* | |
| *June* | |
| *July* | |
| *August* | |
| *September* | |
| *October* | |
| *November* | |
| *December* | |

The names of holidays begin with capital letters, too. Write the name of the holiday below.

*New Year's Day*

 From D'Nealian™ Home/School Activities: Manuscript Practice for Grades 1–3, Copyright © 1986 Scott, Foresman and Company.

# Evaluation

Write the small or lowercase letters. This is a test to see how well you're doing your work. Be careful of the slant, size, and spacing of your letters.

Now write the capital letters.

Now write the small letters without guidelines. You must do it neatly. Make tall letters twice the size of small letters. Watch your slant, size, and spacing.

Now write below the letters you feel you need to practice more.

# Homonyms

Words that sound alike but are spelled differently are called homonyms. Match the homonyms, and write them in the boxes.

| | | |
|---|---|---|
| pair | | bare |
| our | | too, to |
| by | | buy |
| bear | | pare |
| two | | hour |

| | | |
|---|---|---|
| main | | pane |
| meat | | aunt |
| pain | | meet |
| ant | | eight |
| ate | | mane |

| | | |
|---|---|---|
| there | | here |
| hear | | no |
| know | | road |
| right | | their |
| rode | | write |

From D'Nealian™ Home/School Activities: Manuscript Practice for Grades 1–3, Copyright © 1986 Scott, Foresman and Company.

# Road Signs

Below are words used in road signs. These signs are usually printed with all capital letters. Write the sign names using all capital letters. Be careful! Space letters properly.

fog area                 tunnel

airport                    stop

slow                      exit

zoo                       yield

drive safely

road closed

no littering

junction

# Our Solar System

This is a drawing of our solar system. Write the names of the planets in the left column. Then complete the sentences.

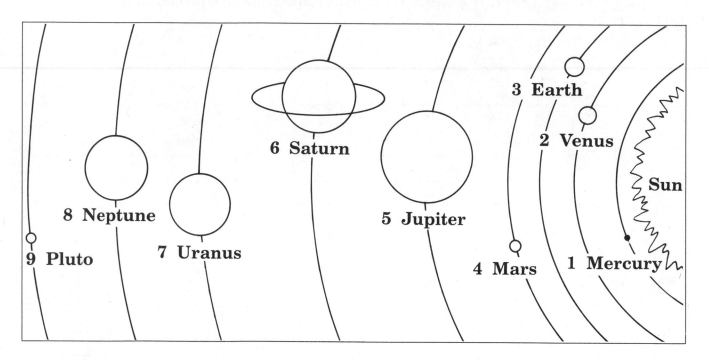

3 Earth

2 Venus

6 Saturn

Sun

8 Neptune

5 Jupiter

9 Pluto    7 Uranus

4 Mars    1 Mercury

We live on planet

The planet closest to the sun is

Most distant from the sun is

The smallest planet is

 From D'Nealian™ Home/School Activities: Manuscript Practice for Grades 1–3, Copyright © 1986 Scott, Foresman and Company.

# Alphabetical Order

Write the words below in alphabetical order.
Use the capital letters to help follow the order.

| into | just | even | quit | most | sail | your |
| open | coat | girl | rope | x-ray | upon | zero |
| able | have | kite | long | nose | very | with |
| bird | dish | frog | twin | past |  |  |

able

# New Meanings

You can change the meaning of many words by adding new endings. Write the words below with the endings **er** and **ed**. Notice how the meanings change. Make all your letters the same size.

| | *er* | *ed* |
|---|---|---|
| *walk* | *walker* | *walked* |
| *buzz* | | |
| *work* | | |
| *call* | | |
| *talk* | | |
| *farm* | | |
| *burn* | | |
| *mark* | | |
| *wash* | | |

From D'Nealian™ Home/School Activities: Manuscript Practice for Grades 1–3, Copyright © 1986 Scott, Foresman and Company.

# Animals

Animals protect themselves in different ways. Write each animal name and what the animal uses to protect itself. Be careful to space words and letters correctly.

| Animal | | Protection | |
|---|---|---|---|
| rattlesnake | deer | claws | tusks |
| scorpion | hawk | fangs | antlers |
| elephant | horse | quills | beak |
| porcupine | bear | hoofs | claws |
| skunk | tiger* | spray | teeth* |
| lobster | | stinger | |

\*tiger                    \*teeth

# Sequencing

Most things happen in a certain order. Something happens first, then something happens next, and then something happens last. Put the things in order. The first one has been done.

water plants, plant seeds, buy seeds, pick tomatoes

*buy seeds, plant seeds, water plants, pick tomatoes*

walk across, look both ways, stop at curb

start motor, put key in, drive away, buckle up

go to school, eat breakfast, wake up, brush teeth

 From D'Nealian™ Home/School Activities: Manuscript Practice for Grades 1–3, Copyright © 1986 Scott, Foresman and Company.

NAME
# Foods

Eating the proper foods keeps you healthy. Talk with your family or teacher about good eating habits. Then write out a menu you'd like for one day's healthy eating. Carefully watch your letter slant, size, and spacing.

| | | | |
|---|---|---|---|
| apple | cheese | honey | pork |
| beans | carrots | juice | potato |
| bacon | celery | lamb | rice |
| banana | chicken | lettuce | soup |
| beef | corn | milk | tomato |
| bread | egg | noodles | turkey |
| butter | fish | orange | waffle |
| cereal | grits | peas | yogurt |

| Breakfast | Lunch | Supper |
|---|---|---|
| | | |
| | | |
| | | |
| | | |
| | | |
| | | |
| | | |
| | | |
| | | |
| | | |

From D'Nealian™ Home/School Activities: Manuscript Practice for Grades 1–3, Copyright © 1986 Scott, Foresman and Company.

# Special Places

Certain things are found in special places. Match each thing with the place where you would expect to find it. Use a capital letter for place names. Carefully watch your small letter spacing, slant, and size.

| planes | books | Airport | Forest | trees |
| Library | Zoo | animals | stores | Shopping Mall |

| Thing | Place Found |
|-------|-------------|
| *books* | *Library* |
| | |
| | |
| | |
| | |

| Hospital | Restaurant | pills | Garage |
| cars | funnies | Newspaper | food |

| Thing | Place Found |
|-------|-------------|
| | |
| | |
| | |
| | |

# Fifty States

A short way to write words is with an abbreviation, like **St.** for **Street** or **Mr.** for **Mister**. The Postal Service uses two letters to abbreviate state names. Below are the fifty state names and their abbreviations. Write each abbreviation in the box by the name. This is practice for writing smaller.

|  | |  | |  | |
|---|---|---|---|---|---|
| Alabama, AL | | Louisiana, LA | | Ohio, OH | |
| Alaska, AK | | Maine, ME | | Oklahoma, OK | |
| Arizona, AZ | | Maryland, MD | | Oregon, OR | |
| Arkansas, AR | | Massachusetts, MA | | Pennsylvania, PA | |
| California, CA | | Michigan, MI | | Rhode Island, RI | |
| Colorado, CO | | Minnesota, MN | | South Carolina, SC | |
| Connecticut, CT | | Mississippi, MS | | South Dakota, SD | |
| Delaware, DE | | Missouri, MO | | Tennessee, TN | |
| Florida, FL | | Montana, MT | | Texas, TX | |
| Georgia, GA | | Nebraska, NE | | Utah, UT | |
| Hawaii, HI | | Nevada, NV | | Vermont, VT | |
| Idaho, ID | | New Hampshire, NH | | Virginia, VA | |
| Illinois, IL | | New Jersey, NJ | | Washington, WA | |
| Indiana, IN | | New Mexico, NM | | West Virginia, WV | |
| Iowa, IA | | New York, NY | | Wisconsin, WI | |
| Kansas, KS | | North Carolina, NC | | Wyoming, WY | |
| Kentucky, KY | | North Dakota, ND | | | |

Write your state's name and abbreviation below.

# Riddles

Here are some riddles for you to answer. A riddle is a joke, so look for the funny ending. You can see the answers at the bottom of the page. Watch your letter and word spacing.

What is the longest word in the English language? Answer:

What question can you never answer with yes? Answer:

How is a bird sitting on a fence like a penny? Answer:

What has four legs and never sits down? Answer:

## Answers

Smiles. There is a mile between the first letter and the last letter.

Are you asleep?

Because it has a head on one side and a tail on the other side.

A table.

 From D'Nealian™ Home/School Activities: Manuscript Practice for Grades 1–3, Copyright © 1986 Scott, Foresman and Company.

# Where Animals Live

Animals spend most of their time in certain places. Write each animal's name in the box where it lives. Be careful of word spacing, letter size, and slant.

**Animals**

elephant

lion

whale

worm

mole

groundhog

shrimp

camel

octopus

elk

crocodile

sheep

lobster

ant

## On the Land

## Under Water

## Under Ground

# The Pledge of Allegiance

Write the Pledge of Allegiance, using small letters instead of the capital letters shown below, but use capital letters for the word **I**, and to begin the words **United**, **States**, **America**, **Republic**, **Nation**, and **God**. Watch your spacing, size, and slant.

I PLEDGE ALLEGIANCE TO THE FLAG

OF THE UNITED STATES OF AMERICA

AND TO THE REPUBLIC FOR WHICH IT STANDS,

ONE NATION, UNDER GOD, INDIVISIBLE,

WITH LIBERTY AND JUSTICE FOR ALL.

# Evaluation

To show that you have learned to print neatly without taking too much time, try the writing test below. Have someone time you. You must be able to write the whole alphabet correctly within three minutes. All letters must be printed with proper space, size, and slant. Use small letters only, not capitals.

Now check to see how well you did.

**First**: Are letters **a**, **b**, **d**, **e**, **g**, **k**, **p**, and **q** closed as they should be or open like these: *a b d e g k p q* ? Take 1 point off for each open letter.

Points off

**Second**: Use a small card or ruler. Place it by the letters **b**, **d**, **f**, **g**, **h**, **j**, **k**, **l**, **p**, **q**, **t**, and **y**. Take one point off for any letter that slants differently from the rest.

Points off

**Third**: All letters should be about the same size, not too tall, short, wide, or thin like these: *h t w b v m k a* Take 1 point off for each letter not made properly.

Points off

**How to score your test:**

No points off     You're a master D'Nealian writer.

1 to 4 points off     You're a good D'Nealian writer.

5 or more points off     Write the alphabet again below, and then recheck your points. Try for no more than 4 points off.

# Cursive Writing

Changing from print to cursive writing is easy. For most lowercase cursive letters, either an up-the-hill or an up-over-the-hill stroke is added to the print letter. Look at and study each letter before writing it to see how the printed letter changes into cursive. You should attempt cursive writing only after you have **mastered print**, with proper slant, spacing, and letter size. Print well first, and your cursive writing will be excellent.

Because this book is mainly a manuscript printing book, little space is provided for cursive practice. Capital letters are shown on this page. The last pages will show how print switches to cursive writing.

Use this space to practice cursive capitals.

From D'Nealian™ Home/School Activities: Manuscript Practice for Grades 1–3, Copyright © 1986 Scott, Foresman and Company.

NAME

# Cursive Practice

Study each letter before writing it to see how it changes. For letters **a**, **d**, **c**, **m**, **n**, and **x**, add an up-over-the-hill stroke like this:    . Start at the dot, and follow the arrow.

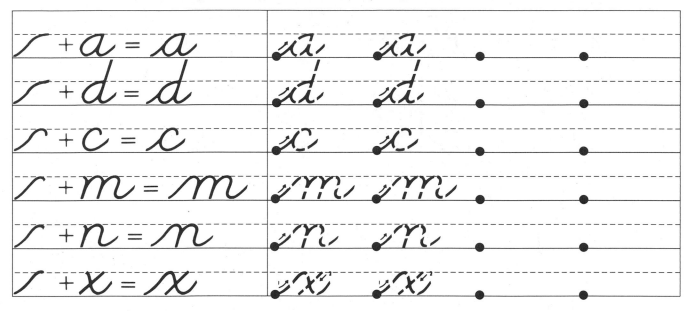

Write these connected letter groups.

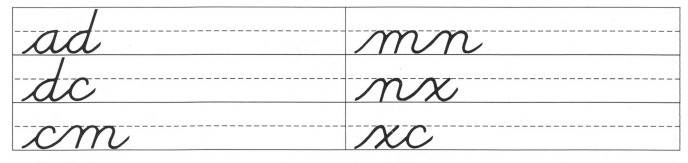

Practice writing the words below.

*add*

*dad*

*man*

*ax*

*can*

# Cursive Practice

Letters **o**, **g**, **q**, **v**, **y**, and **z** all begin with an up-over-the-hill stroke: ⌢. Be careful to keep the bottom stroke on **g**, **q**, **y**, and **z** straight, not like these: _g_ _q_ _y_ _z_

Write these connected letter groups.

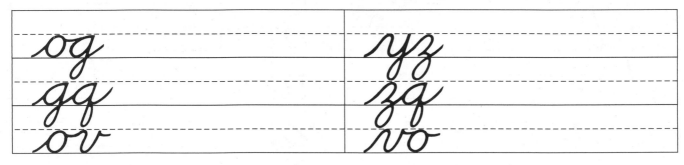

Practice writing these words.

*zoo*

*yam*

*go*

*yo-yo*

*van*

From D'Nealian™ Home/School Activities: Manuscript Practice for Grades 1–3, Copyright © 1986 Scott, Foresman and Company.

# Cursive Practice

These letters start with an up-the-hill stroke, like this:    . Be careful of letter size, slant, and spacing.

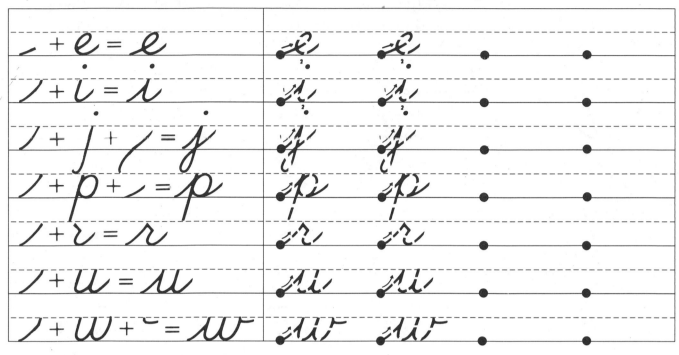

Write these connected letter groups.

Write these words. Be careful of letter spacing.

# Cursive Practice

These letters also begin with an up-the-hill stroke. They take two spaces to write except for letter **s**. To make a good letter **s**, come straight down after the up-the-hill stroke, then curve back in, and add a monkey tail.

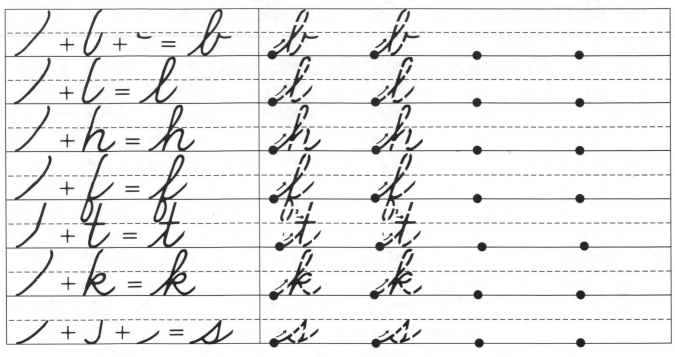

| | | | |
|---|---|---|---|
| / + $l$ + ˘ = $b$ | $b$ | $b$ | |
| / + $l$ = $l$ | $l$ | $l$ | |
| / + $h$ = $h$ | $h$ | $h$ | |
| / + $f$ = $f$ | $f$ | $f$ | |
| / + $t$ = $t$ | $t$ | $t$ | |
| / + $k$ = $k$ | $k$ | $k$ | |
| / + $J$ + ⌣ = $s$ | $s$ | $s$ | |

Write these connected letter groups.

| | |
|---|---|
| $bl$ | $tk$ |
| $lh$ | $fl$ |
| $hf$ | $lt$ |
| $sl$ | $sh$ |

Practice writing the words below.

$bush$

$full$

$kite$

 From D'Nealian™ Home/School Activities: Manuscript Practice for Grades 1–3, Copyright © 1986 Scott, Foresman and Company.

NAME

NAME

From **D'Nealian™ Home/School Activities: Manuscript Practice for Grades 1–3**, Copyright © 1986 Scott, Foresman and Company.